DEREK HEADLEY

Excel Formulas & Pivot Tables

Basic knowledge for the beginner in a language you can understand

First edition

This book was professionally typeset on Reedsy.
Find out more at reedsy.com

Contents

1

Introduction

I decided to write this book to help people better understand a few of the big skills in Excel that employers look for, as well as use in your personal life to help keep track of various things. While working with other people who have not had the exposure to Excel that I have, it's become evident they fail to understand how to utilize these tools and features because of a couple reasons.

1. They are not working in Excel on a consistent basis to help them retain what they do learn.
2. The descriptions of arguments within formulas are not clear enough for most people to understand.
3. A lot of the videos and instruction guides out there tell you how to do something in Excel, but fail to break down the process in general enough terms that allow people to be able to use those tools and functions in other scenarios besides the example given.
4. Most of the videos and blogs out there speak to you as if you are a seasoned veteran in the world of Excel and its formulas, functions, and pivot table design. This does not help the average person who might have some experience with Excel, but not enough to follow

the logic behind these things and the way they work.

Let me give you a little background on myself and my experience with Excel. I do not consider myself an expert in any way shape or form, as a matter of fact, I know there is still a ton for me to learn in Excel, and I try to learn something new everyday. I have only gone through one Excel training session that was provided by the company I was working for at the time, and that was back in the late 90's or early 2000's. I have always been fascinated with utilizing Excel as a tool both in the workplace and in my personal life as I feel it's a great resource for so many different things. Everything I know about Excel has been self taught through observation, trial and error, and research online. I'm not ashamed to admit that I will search Google and Youtube for hours to find a solution to something I'm trying to do in Excel, and you shouldn't be afraid to utilize Google and Youtube to search for things you want to learn as well. There is an endless amount of resources out there to help you accomplish what you are trying to achieve.

There is also an endless supply of different books out there to help you understand probably anything and everything there is to know about Excel. So what makes my book any different from the others available to you? I have experience teaching everyday people how to utilize Excel to create reports, become familiar with different formulas and functions to where they understand what they're doing with them and not just how to do them to accomplish the one task they are currently working on, and have watched them get faster and more comfortable within Excel because they finally have an understanding of what they are doing in there. This is not one of those books that claim to cover everything you can do within Excel, I've intentionally kept it short and focused so it's not daunting.

My goal with this book is to help as many people as possible get a better understanding and become more comfortable with a few key things to know in Excel that will get your skills more noticed at work or in interviews, and give you a jumping off point to explore more in Excel in order to further your knowledge.

So why should you buy this book if you can do everything I've done yourself? That's a great question because if I can get to a point where I can teach people how to use Excel simply by my drive to learn as much about it on my own utilizing all free resources out there then why can't you? The answer is "You Can", if you want to take the time and effort to find the resources, use trial and error to figure things out, etc. Remember that I said I took one training course back in the late 90's or early 2000's, and as I'm writing this book in 2024 that should give you an idea of how long I've been at this. Hopefully by going through this book I can save you all the time it's taken me to get where I am with my Excel knowledge, and time is money.

So let's dive in and get started on getting you some helpful knowledge using Microsoft Excel basics to jump start your journey.

*** Some functions and formulas may not be available to you depending on what version of Excel you are using, and whether you are using Excel in your internet browser or using the actual program.*

2

Understanding the Excel Layout and Format

When you open an Excel document, you are opening what is referred to as a "Workbook". Within each Workbook are tabs at the bottom for sheets known as "Spreadsheets". These spreadsheets are laid out like a table of "Cells" with column labels using letters to differentiate between each column, and rows with numerical labels to differentiate each row. In the top left of the table you will see a dropdown box called the "Name Box", this gives you the location of the cell you are working in by column and row (In the example below the Name Box is displaying "A1" indicating your currently in the cell located in the first row and first column of the workbook).

All of your data gets organized in this table within the individual cells, meaning each cell should contain a different piece of data. You can decide exactly how you want that layout to look by what data you would like to have displayed vertically (up and down in the columns) and what data you would like to have lined up horizontally (side to side in the rows). You can also format individual cells or groups of cells by highlighting them and right clicking on your mouse, then selecting "Format Cells". Sometimes you are manually keying all of your data in the spreadsheet like this, and sometimes you are either pulling the data into Excel from another source or you are copying and pasting the data into Excel from a different source or spreadsheet. In some cases the data may not already be formatted the way you would like it, or a lot times will contain data you do not need and/or could be missing data necessary for your spreadsheet, and this is where formulas and pivot tables will come in handy to help you reorganize all the data into a format best suited to display a more concise version.

What you've created by importing data, manually keying data, or copying and pasting data into your spreadsheet is a table outline or a dataset. One option you have here is to turn that into an actual "Table" which will give all of your headers a filter button so you can filter the information as needed. This also creates the table to be expandable by dragging the bottom right corner of the table, if you need to start adding additional rows or columns of data. This option does not give you totals for rows or columns and does not let you easily reorganize columns and rows without cutting and pasting or dragging. This does provide a quick and easy way to make the data look presentable with options to sort the data as needed if you need to do something on the fly, utilizing the pivot table and formulas will help you accomplish the things a table lacks to give your data a more concise and finished look.

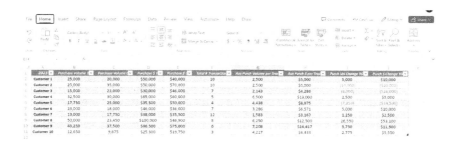

3

Fundamental Formula and Function Information

At the very top of Excel you have a row of tabs, one of which is labeled "Formulas", and if you click on that tab the toolbar will give you a list of different function options. These are all preset formulas with various functions they provide, this will have practically every function you could need to get the information out the data you are seeking. The options in this tab are extremely useful if you know what you are looking for and can understand what the description of the function is telling you it does (descriptions can be obtained by hovering your mouse over the function name).

One thing you will learn about Excel if you don't already know it, is there are numerous ways to get the same information within the program. For example, you can select a function from the options in the "Formulas" tab to guide you on creating your formula, or you can type out the formula inside the cell itself if you know it, or even what it starts with (as you start typing out a formula manually in a cell you will get a pop up list with all the functions, containing whatever you've typed out in the cell, within the name of the function, you can double click on the function name from that list to insert it in the cell if you want). With that being said, don't get discouraged if you're unable to figure something out in Excel based on what one person teaches you because there are many other options out there to get the result you're looking for, you just have to find the method that works for you.

To manually type a formula into a cell always start with the equals sign (=), this indicates to Excel you are putting a formula in the cell so it knows what to expect next. I've found that very often it's quicker for me to use this method to do simple math equations, i.e. getting percentages, simple addition, subtraction, multiplication, and division among a small group of cells. The typed out formula would look something like the examples below:

- =A1/B1
- =A1*B1
- =A1-B1
- =A1+B1

You can also start typing out an already preset formula if you know it and then double click it from the list that pops up to have it start filling in within the cell, see example below:

FUNDAMENTAL FORMULA AND FUNCTION INFORMATION

G14   =sum

Chase Volume 1	Purchase Volume 2	Purchase $ T	Purchase $ L	Total # Transaction	Ave Purch Volume per Tra	Ave Purch $ per Tran	Purch Vol Change V3	Purch $ Change Yr
17,750	25,000	$55,500	$50,000	4	4,438	$8,875	(2,250)	($14,500)
23,000	18,000	$46,000	$36,000	7	3,286	$6,571	5,000	$10,000
19,000	17,750	$38,000	$35,500	12	1,583	$3,167	1,250	$2,500
50,000	23,450	$100,000	$46,900	8	6,250	$12,500	26,550	$53,100
43,250	37,500	$86,500	$75,000	6	7,208	$14,417	5,750	$11,500
12,650	9,875	$25,300	$19,750	3	4,217	$8,433	2,775	$5,550

=sum

SUM(table1[Ave Purch Volume per Tran]) = 40,524

○ SUM

○ SUMIF

○ SUMIFS

Give feedback

Sheet1

4

Most Useful Basic Formulas

There are over 300 formulas in Excel and while it would be nice to know and be able to utilize all of them, let's start with some of the most useful basic formulas to get you started. You may have seen or even used some of these formulas before, but hopefully there are a few you can learn that will help achieve your goals within Excel. The list below contains some of the most useful formulas and what they do:

- COUNTA() - This counts the number of cells within a specified range that are not blank
- COUNTIF(), SUMIF() - These count or add the cells within a specified range that meet your given criteria [Determines if the value of a cell is TRUE or FALSE based on your criteria]
- AVERAGE() - This will return the average of a given range of cells
- CONCAT() - This will combine the string of selected cells
- Example: If you have First Name in one cell and Last Name in another cell you can use the CONCAT formula in a third cell to combine the first and last name into that cell
- Note: This formula combines the selected cells in the order you

select them, so in the example above you have to select the cell with the first name first and the cell with the last name second

- IFERROR(), IFNA() - These can be used before another formula to allow you to determine what value to return if there is an error or the result of the formula is #N/A
- Example: When dealing with numerical values if you would rather see a 0 instead of the #N/A when the formula does not find a value to return you can use this function and designate the "0" to be returned if the value is not found
- TODAY() - This will return the current date today in a date format (M/D/YYYY)
- PROPER() - This is a useful formula if you are not the greatest at spelling or capitalizing proper nouns
- This function will take any text in the selected cell range and correct the spelling and proper grammar
- Example: You type a first name in one cell and a last name in another cell but use all lower case lettering; Use this formula selecting those cells and it will change them to the proper capitalization

Cell 1 = *john*, Cell 2 = *smith*, the correction made with this formula will change those cells to read as follows, Cell 1 = *John*, Cell 2 = *Smith*

5

Using and Understanding Lookup Formulas and Functions

L ookup formulas are one of the most useful tools within Excel, these help you lookup information from other sheets, workbooks, and tables and bring them into the sheet or table you are currently working on. This will save you a ton of time from having to search and find that data yourself and then either copying and pasting, or entering the information into the area needed making you infinitely more efficient.

There are numerous ways to achieve this utilizing different formulas or combined functions within Excel. Here we will cover a couple of the more common lookup formulas and discuss the difference between them so you can decide which one will best suit your needs. We will touch on vlookups, xlookups, and the filter formula. Here we will also look at some additional formulas to combine with lookup formulas to make your data set more presentable and look more put together.

VLOOKUP

VLOOKUPs search through a specified range of cells using a fixed value to find a matching value within that range. Once found, it retrieves a value from the same row, based on the column index you specify in the formula. The standard vlookup formula is below:

=VLOOKUP(lookup value, table array, column index number, range lookup)

- **Lookup value** = the cell in the data set you're working in containing the value you need the formula to look for in the other sheet, workbook, or table you're retrieving the data from
- **Table array** = the range of cells or table name you would like the formula look in to pull the data you need to bring over to the current data set you're working in
- **Column index number** = the column number in the table array containing the data you are trying to return to your data set {count the number of columns from left to right, including the column containing your lookup value, put that number in the formula, i.e. 1, 2, 3, 4, etc.}
- **Range lookup** = this is a true/false value indicating if you would like the lookup value to be an exact match, or the closest match possible. True {closest match possible}, False {exact match}
- *** Vlookups can only search from left to right, this means the table array must be structured in a way that has the column containing the lookup value to the left of the column index number you are retrieving data from*

Sample Data Set

2023	Address	City	State	Zip	Phone Number
Customer 1	123 Main Rd	Nowhereville	AL	12345	555-123-4567
Customer 2	123 Main Rd	Nowhereville	AR	12345	555-123-4567
Customer 3	123 Main Rd	Nowhereville	NV	12345	555-123-4567
Customer 4	123 Main Rd	Nowhereville	TX	12345	555-123-4567
Customer 5	123 Main Rd	Nowhereville	NY	12345	555-123-4567
Customer 6	123 Main Rd	Nowhereville	NJ	12345	555-123-4567
Customer 7	123 Main Rd	Nowhereville	OR	12345	555-123-4567
Customer 8	123 Main Rd	Nowhereville	AZ	12345	555-123-4567
Customer 9	123 Main Rd	Nowhereville	WY	12345	555-123-4567
Customer 10	123 Main Rd	Nowhereville	MN	12345	555-123-4567

Sample Table Array

2023	Purchase Volume T	Purchase Volume L	Purchase $ T	Purchase $ L	Total # Transaction	Ave Purch Volume per Tran	Ave Purch $ per Tran	Purch Vol Change TD	Purch $ Change TD
Customer 1	25,000	20,000	$50,000	$40,000	10	2,500	$5,000	5,000	$10,000
Customer 2	25,000	35,000	$50,000	$70,000	10	3,500	$5,000	(10,000)	$(20,000)
Customer 3	15,000	23,000	$30,000	$46,000	7	2,143	$4,286	(8,000)	$(16,000)
Customer 4	32,500	30,000	$65,000	$60,000	5	6,500	$13,000	2,500	$5,000
Customer 5	17,750	25,000	$35,500	$50,000	4	4,438	$8,875	(7,250)	$(14,500)
Customer 6	23,000	18,000	$46,000	$36,000	7	3,286	$6,571	5,000	$10,000
Customer 7	19,000	17,750	$38,000	$35,500	12	1,583	$3,167	1,250	$2,500
Customer 8	50,000	23,450	$100,000	$46,900	8	6,250	$12,500	26,550	$53,100
Customer 9	43,250	37,500	$86,500	$75,000	6	7,208	$14,417	5,750	$11,500
Customer 10	12,650	9,875	$25,300	$19,750	3	4,217	$8,433	2,775	$5,550
Totals	263,150	239,575	$526,300	$479,150	72	3,655	$7,310	23,575	$47,150

Example: Using the sample tables above, if you use a vlookup to find the average purchase dollars per transaction for customer 3, then your formula would look like this;

=VLOOKUP(A4,'Sample Table Array'A1:J12,8,FALSE)

Here A4 refers to the cell containing the value we are looking for in the table array, 'Sample Table Array'A1:J12 is showing the table in which the formula is looking to match the lookup value and return a value from, 8 is the column index number containing the information we are looking to return, FALSE is telling the formula we need an exact match.

Vlookup does not have an option built into the formula arguments to return a value of your choosing if no lookup value is found like the xlookup (If Not Found) or filter formula (If Empty) argument fields. You can get around this by using the "IFERROR" function prior to the vlookup formula where you include the value to return if the lookup value is not found after the vlookup formula:

=IFERROR(VLOOKUP(A4,'Sample Table Array'A1:J12,8,FALSE)," ")

Here the "IFERROR" return value is " " which will return a blank if the lookup value is not found. You can insert anything you would like in between those quotation marks to have as the return value, this can be text or numerical (i.e. "Not Found", or "0").

XLOOKUP

Xlookups are very similar to Vlookups, however, they offer a little more flexibility. Instead of using a table array to look for a value to return, the xlookup uses a lookup array and a return array which doesn't require the table of data to be in any certain order (remember, vlookups can only search left to right for data requiring the lookup value to be to the left of the return value). The standard xlookup formula is below:

=XLOOKUP(lookup value, lookup array, return array)

- **Lookup Value** = the cell in the data set you're working in containing the value you need the formula to look for in the other sheet, workbook, or table you're retrieving the data from
- **Lookup Array** = the array or range of cells to search for the lookup value in
- **Return Array** = the array or range of cells containing the return value(s) you are searching for

15

- ***If Not Found*** = what you designate the formula to return in the case the lookup value is not found (i.e. could be a value such as '0' or text such as 'Not Found'), if not designated the default is "#N/A"
- ***Match Mode*** = this is the lookup value match type, see options below
- 0 = Exact Match, if an exact lookup value match is not found, then it returns what you designate in the '*If Not Found*' argument of the formula (Default)
- -1 = If an exact match is not found then it matches the next smaller value
- 1 = If an exact match is not found then it matches the next larger value
- 2 = Wildcard, is where *, ?, ~ have a special meaning and are usually used to find either partial matches or similar matches
- ***Search Mode*** = the order in which the formula searches for the lookup value, see options below:
- 1 = start the search at the first item and move first to last
- -1 = reverse search starting at the last item and moving last to first
- 2 = binary search requiring the lookup array to be in ascending order, if not in ascending order the formula will return an error
- -2 = binary search requiring the lookup array to be in descending order, if not in descending order the formula will return an error

Denotes an optional argument, these are not required for the formula to work

Example: Using the same sample data set and same sample table array as the vlookup scenario above, the xlookup formula to use for the same results as the vlookup example would be as follows:

=XLOOKUP(A4,'Sample Table Array'A2:A11,'Sample Table Array'H2:H11)

Here A4 refers to the cell containing the value you are looking for in the table array, 'Sample Table Array'A1:A11 is the column of cells where you are looking to match your lookup value, 'Sample Table Array'H2:H11 is the column of cells containing the information you are trying to return.

FILTER

The filter function allows you to search a range of cells and return all results matching the criteria you set. This is useful when you have more than one entry for the same criteria, where the vlookup and xlookup will only return a single value to you, the filter function returns all values within the specified range to you. The standard filter formula will look like this:

=FILTER(Array, Include)

- **Array** = the range of cells or table name you would like the formula look in to pull the data you need to bring over to the current data set you're working in
- **Include** = the range of cells you want to match with your set criteria
- ***If Empty*** = what you designate the formula to return in the case the lookup value is not found

Denotes an optional argument, these are not required for the formula to work

Year	Product	Sales	Returns	Sales $	Return $
2020	Dairy	25	5	$125	$25
2020	Electronics	75	3	$1,500	$60
2020	Clothing	13	2	$195	$80
2020	Pet Care	10	1	$30	$3
2021	Dairy	10	1	$50	$5
2021	Electronics	13	2	$260	$40
2021	Clothing	75	3	$1,125	$45
2021	Pet Care	25	5	$75	$15
2022	Dairy	32	4	$160	$20
2022	Electronics	54	6	$1,080	$120
2022	Clothing	27	8	$405	$120
2022	Pet Care	16	10	$48	$30
2023	Dairy	16	10	$80	$50
2023	Electronics	27	8	$540	$160
2023	Clothing	54	6	$810	$90

Selection	Year	Product	Sales	Returns	Sales $	Return $
Electronics	2020	Electronics	75	3	1500	60
	2021	Electronics	13	2	260	40
	2022	Electronics	54	6	1080	120
	2023	Electronics	27	8	540	160

Example: In the above sample we are trying to get all the information for "Electronics" including the year, sales & return volume, and sales & return dollars. As you can see in the table there are multiple entries for "Electronics", using a vlookup or xlookup will only get you data from one entry, but not all entries. In this case we can use the following filter formula to get the results from all entries:

=FILTER(A2:F17,B2:B17=H2)

This formula would be entered in cell I2 where 'A2:F17' is referring to the table we are pulling information from, 'B2:B17' is the column of cells where we are looking to match our lookup value, and 'H2' is our lookup value. If we were to change the value in cell H2 then the formula would change its lookup value to meet that criteria and pull in the information only related to that value.

There are many other functions that can be combined with the filter function that will help limit the return data, for example, if you only want certain columns (such as Sales $) in the table to be returned you can use the the preceding function of "CHOOSECOLS", then after the the filter formula you would add the column index number of the columns you want to display:

=CHOOSECOLS(FILTER(A2:F17,B2:B17=H2),5)

Or, if you want to display your results vertically instead of horizontally, you could use the "TRANSPOSE" function before the filter formula:

=TRANSPOSE(FILTER(A2:F17,B2:B17=H2))

6

Pivot Tables

Pivot tables are another area which can seem overwhelming and intimidating for users who have not had very much exposure to Excel or pivot tables themselves. They are actually fairly easy to put together and use if you understand the basics behind them. In this chapter we will cover some of the basics of pivot tables to get you more comfortable creating and utilizing them, along with how they can be useful and efficient to use.

To get started creating a pivot table you will want to highlight all of the rows and columns within your data set or table containing the information you are working with. From there select the "Insert" tab at the top of the worksheet and choose the "Pivot Table" option on the far left and then "From Table/Range" from the dropdown. You will then get a popup and in the "Table/Range" field it should already have your range selected, and here you can choose to insert the pivot table into a new worksheet, or place it in a certain area within an existing worksheet by selecting the cell in that worksheet where you would like the pivot table to be placed. Once you have completed that pop up you will be taken to the "Field List" to select the information you want displayed in the pivot table.

Field List

The field list collects all the fields in your range or table and allows you to use all or some of them in the pivot table. There are four areas in the field list where your fields can be placed, and you can place one or more fields in these areas:

- Filters - This area allows you to filter your results based on selections of the different fields within that area
- Columns - This area allows you to show what fields will be displayed horizontally across the pivot table
- Rows - This area allow you to show what fields will be displayed vertically within the pivot table
- Values - This is the area where the data will be displayed in the pivot table
- There are numerous ways to summarize the field values in this area, below are the most commonly used summaries:
- Sum - Displays the total value in the field
- Count - Displays the total number of values in the field
- Average - Displays the average of the values in the field
- Max - Displays the largest value in the field
- Min - Displays the lowest value in the field

So let's say you have a data set showing different regions and the products those stores sell. The data set includes numerous data points, but you need to send a file to your boss with only the sales dollars. You could go through and hide rows and columns in the worksheet you are currently working in, or create a pivot table to show just the sales dollars by region and by product, then copy and paste that pivot table into a fresh workbook to send over. See the example below with how to set the field list to show exactly what you are looking for.

Sample Data Set

	A	B	C	D	E	F	G	H
1	Sales Area	Product Description	2024 Sales Volum	2024 Sales Dollar	2024 Return Volum	2024 Return Dollar	2024 Return % Volum	2024 Return % Dollar
2	Central	Electronics	2,630	$10,343	174	$694	7%	7%
3	Central	Childrens clothes	1,235	$7,722	86	$551	7%	7%
4	Central	Pet Supplies	557	$2,188	79	$311	14%	14%
5	Central	Mens Wear	2,995	$16,130	54	$327	2%	2%
6	Central	Womens Wear	761	$4,661	102	$624	13%	13%
7	Midwest	Electronics	5,330	$20,733	665	$2,606	13%	13%
8	Midwest	Childrens clothes	7,198	$41,502	155	$891	2%	2%
9	Midwest	Pet Supplies	749	$2,915	220	$857	29%	29%
10	Midwest	Mens Wear	5,266	$27,630	503	$2,641	10%	10%
11	Midwest	Womens Wear	3,456	$19,156	293	$1,628	8%	8%
12	East	Electronics	8,096	$32,538	871	$3,507	11%	11%
13	East	Pet Supplies	1,577	$6,338	163	$656	10%	10%
14	East	Mens Wear	5,908	$33,137	378	$2,123	6%	6%
15	East	Womens Wear	934	$5,928	137	$869	15%	15%
16	North	Electronics	5,079	$16,559	289	$941	6%	6%
17	North	Childrens clothes	3,597	$16,008	53	$236	1%	1%
18	North	Pet Supplies	1,825	$4,973	207	$874	14%	14%
19	North	Mens Wear	4,424	$16,947	257	$983	6%	6%
20	North	Womens Wear	2,376	$11,048	45	$209	2%	2%
21	South	Electronics	9,574	$38,493	568	$2,285	6%	6%
22	South	Pet Supplies	2,085	$8,379	214	$861	10%	10%
23	South	Mens Wear	7,502	$42,079	206	$1,157	3%	3%
24	South	Womens Wear	1,478	$9,386	42	$266	3%	3%

When creating your pivot table you would set the field list as follows

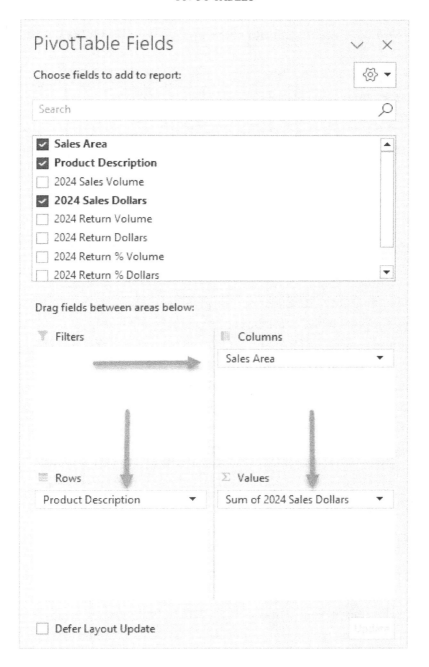

And your results should show up like the pivot table below

Sum of 2024 Sales Dollars	Column Labels					
Row Labels	Central	East	Midwest	North	South	Grand Total
Childrens clothes	$7,721.64		$41,502.49	$16,007.69		$65,231.82
Electronics	$10,342.76	$32,537.52	$20,733.28	$16,558.50	$38,492.82	$118,664.88
Mens Wear	$18,129.62	$33,137.00	$27,630.18	$16,947.25	$42,079.14	$137,923.19
Pet Supplies	$2,188.42	$6,337.67	$2,914.78	$4,973.07	$8,379.07	$24,793.01
Womens Wear	$4,681.04	$5,928.20	$19,158.24	$11,047.60	$9,386.22	$50,201.30
Grand Total	$43,063.48	$77,940.39	$111,938.97	$65,534.11	$98,337.25	$396,814.20

Additional Pivot Table Information

A few things to point out about the pivot table above, this is the default look for pivot tables (with the exception of the formatting of the data to put it in a currency form, the default cell format is "General", I changed this to "Currency"). You can also see the drop down filter next to "Row Labels" and "Column Labels", this allows you to filter by anything within those fields, i.e. if you want to just show the sales dollars for electronics in the south region you could filter the rows to show only electronics and filter the columns to show only the south region.

You can also adjust the design of the pivot table by selecting the "Design" tab at the top right. Here you can take away the grand totals for either/or the rows and columns, change the report layout, and set your subtotals as well. The pivot table defaults to the blue color design, but in this tab you can also change the color and border designs.

Another tab at your disposal is the "PivotTable Analyze" tab up top. Here you can take your pivot table and make charts from it, or see what charts Excel recommends based on your data. You can also change your data source (where the pivot table is pulling information from), and access the field settings and pivot table options, as well as name the pivot table if you would like. There are some more advanced options on this tab such as "Insert Slicer" and "Insert Timeline", and you can play around with those, but there is more training you would want to get in order to take full advantage of those options.

7

Function Terms & Categories

Function & Formula Terms	Description
Functions	Predefined formulas that perform calculations using specific values (arguments), e.g., SUM(), AVERAGE(), VLOOKUP(). - These are the formulas Excel already has set up for you.
Arguments	The values that functions need to perform calculations, enclosed in parentheses, e.g., SUM(A1:A10) where A1:A10 is the argument.
Cell Reference	Refers to a specific cell or range of cells used in a formula, can be relative (A1), absolute (A1), or mixed (A$1, $A1). - In this case the "$" indicates a fixed row, column or cell, in other words that stays the same anywhere you drag or move that formula.
Operators	Symbols that define the type of calculation, including arithmetic (+, -, *, /, ^), comparison (=, <>, >, <, >=, <=), and text concatenation (&).
Constants	Numbers or text values entered directly into a formula, such as 2 or "Hello".
Array Formulas	Formulas that perform multiple calculations on one or more items in an array, returning single or multiple results, entered with Ctrl+Shift+Enter.
Named Ranges	A name that refers to one or more cells, which can be used in formulas instead of cell references, e.g., naming A1:A10 as "Sales" and using Sales in a formula.
Conditional Logic	Functions that perform actions based on conditions, such as IF(), AND(), OR(), NOT().
Error Values	Special values returned when Excel cannot calculate a formula, e.g., #DIV/0!, #N/A, #NAME?, #NULL!, #NUM!, #REF!, #VALUE!
Array Constants	Sets of constants used within array formulas, enclosed in braces {}, e.g., {1,2,3}.

FUNCTION TERMS & CATEGORIES

Function Categories	Functions
Basic Math	SUM(), AVERAGE(), MIN(), MAX(), SUMPRODUCT()
Statistical	COUNT(), COUNTA(), COUNTBLANK(), AVERAGEIF(), MEDIAN(), MODE(), STDEV(), VAR()
Financial	PV(), FV(), NPV(), IRR(), PMT(), RATE(), XNPV(), XIRR()
Text	LEFT(), RIGHT(), MID(), LEN(), TRIM(), UPPER(), LOWER(), CONCATENATE()
Date and Time	NOW(), TODAY(), DATE(), DAY(), MONTH(), YEAR(), DAYS(), EDATE()
Lookup & Reference	VLOOKUP(), HLOOKUP(), INDEX(), MATCH(), OFFSET(), INDIRECT()
Logical	IF(), AND(), OR(), NOT(), IFERROR(), IFS(), SWITCH()
Information	ISBLANK(), ISNUMBER(), ISTEXT(), ISERROR(), TYPE()
Array	ARRAYFORMULA(), TRANSPOSE(), FREQUENCY(), UNIQUE(), SEQUENCE()

8

Conclusion

E xcel can be very intimidating and overwhelming, especially if you are not utilizing it on a regular basis. I have learned everything I know just by deciding what I would like to accomplish and figuring out how to get it done by searching google, youtube, observing others working within the application, and most importantly just diving in and playing around in Excel. I hope this short book has simplified things for you and given you a better understanding of how functions, formulas, and pivot tables work, along with how to utilize them to achieve your desired results.

I appreciate you taking a look at the book and reading through its content. If you enjoyed this book and/or feel like it helped you learn more about using those features in Excel please recommend to anyone who you think would benefit from it, and please leave a review to help get it out to others who it might help.

9

References:

- *Formulas and functions - Microsoft Support.* (n.d.). https://support.microsoft.com/en-us/office/formulas-and-functions-294d9486-b332-48ed-b489-abe7d0f9eda9?ns=EXCEL&version=90

www.ingramcontent.com/pod-product-compliance
Lightning Source LLC
LaVergne TN
LVHW022126060326
832903LV00063B/4789